MW00785157

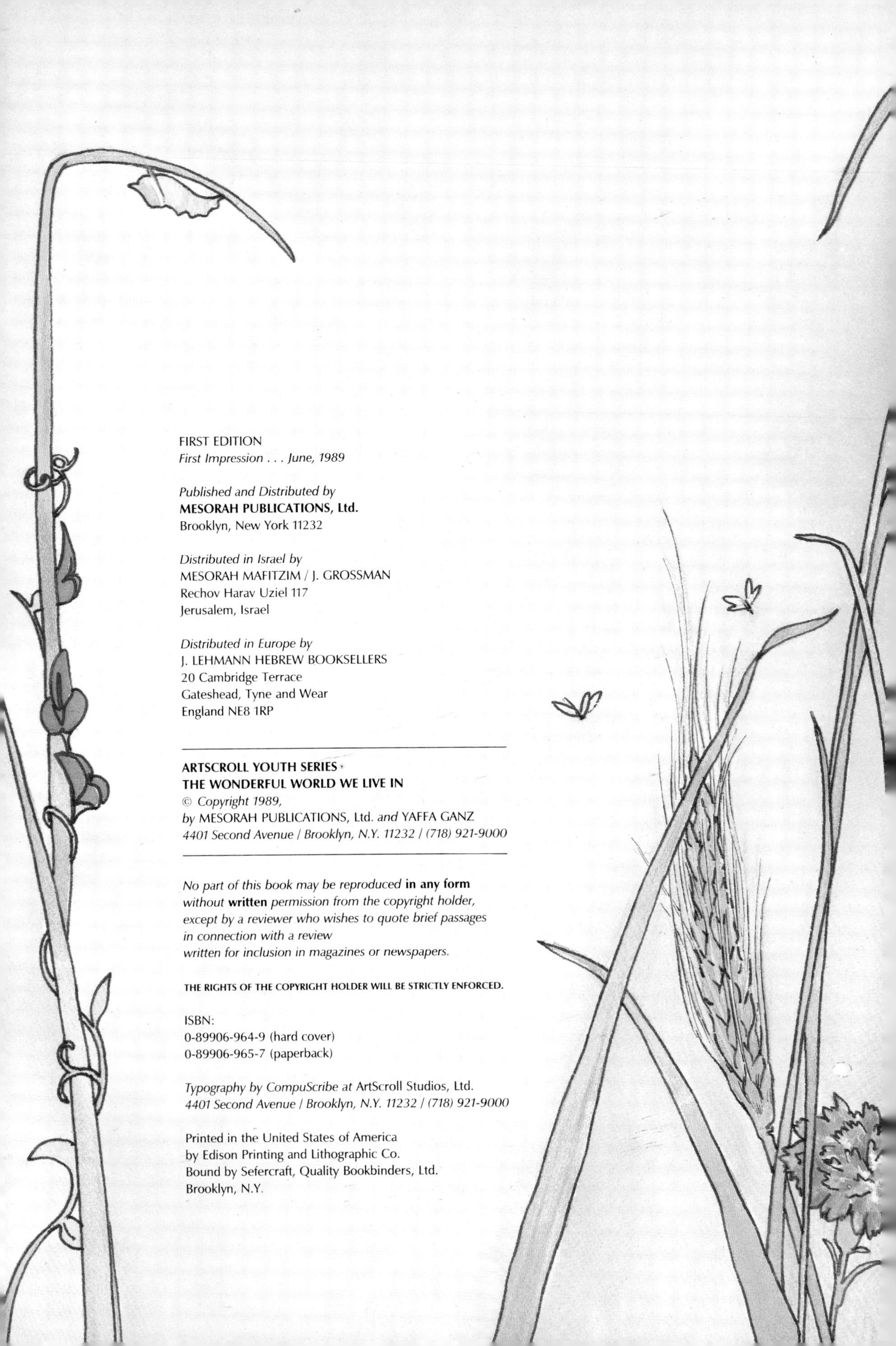

FIRST EDITION
First Impression . . . June, 1989

Published and Distributed by
MESORAH PUBLICATIONS, Ltd.
Brooklyn, New York 11232

Distributed in Israel by
MESORAH MAFITZIM / J. GROSSMAN
Rechov Harav Uziel 117
Jerusalem, Israel

Distributed in Europe by
J. LEHMANN HEBREW BOOKSELLERS
20 Cambridge Terrace
Gateshead, Tyne and Wear
England NE8 1RP

ARTSCROLL YOUTH SERIES
THE WONDERFUL WORLD WE LIVE IN

ISBN:
0-89906-964-9 (hard cover)
0-89906-965-7 (paperback)

Typography by CompuScribe at ArtScroll Studios, Ltd.
4401 Second Avenue / Brooklyn, N.Y. 11232 / (718) 921-9000

Printed in the United States of America
by Edison Printing and Lithographic Co.
Bound by Sefercraft, Quality Bookbinders, Ltd.
Brooklyn, N.Y.

To my husband

שֶׁיִּחְיֶה לְאֹרֶךְ יָמִים טוֹבִים אָמֵן

DID YOU EVER WONDER how the mountains grew so high? Or why water feels so wet? Or where the colors of a dewy rainbow go when they disappear from the sky?

Did you ever see a butterfly crawl out of a cocoon? Or watch a tiny seed attached to a silken parachute blow away in the wind? Or hold a brand new, warm, squiggly puppy, just now born?

Did you ever wonder about all of the many amazing things G-d created?

Long long ago, when David Hamelech looked at the wonderful world we live in, he wrote in the Book of *Tehillim:*

בָּרְכִי נַפְשִׁי אֶת ה', ה' אֱלֹקַי גָּדַלְתָּ מְּאֹד,
הוֹד וְהָדָר לָבָשְׁתָּ.

My soul will bless Hashem.
Hashem, my G-d, You are very, very great.
You are clothed in glory and majesty.

What is inky black but full of light? The nighttime sky, of course. It is full of stars, millions and millions of them, more than anyone can possibly count. During the day, when the sun is shining, it's too bright to see the stars. But at night, the sky is like a sheet of black velvet, glittering with tiny diamonds.

Not everything in the sky is a star. There are planets and comets and faraway suns and moons too. Big and small, reddish and blue, and shining white. How many of them there are, and how small they look. But how big and beautiful they make the sky!

Hashem made the sun and the moon and the stars on the fourth day of Creation. And he promised Avraham Avinu that one day, the Jewish people will be as numerous as the stars in the sky. Just as no one can count the stars, no one will be able to count us either!

עֹטֶה אוֹר כַּשַּׂלְמָה, נוֹטֶה שָׁמַיִם כַּיְרִיעָה.

You clothe the world in a robe of light. You spread the heavens out like a curtain.

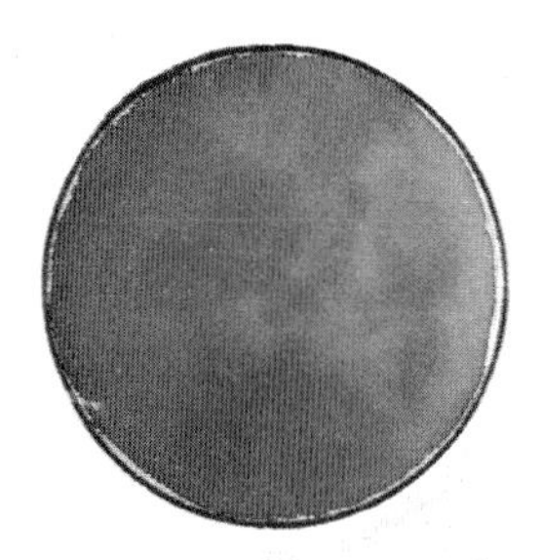

Each morning, a wonderful thing happens. The sun rises in the sky, the world fills with light, and a new day begins!

Our sun is a great burning star far away in the sky. It gives light and heat to the entire world, and it makes everything grow — including you! It is so bright that you cannot look at it without hurting your eyes. It even gives light to the moon. And it is so hot that it melts the snow and dries up the rain. Without the sun, all the oceans and lakes would freeze and the world would become covered with ice.

Once, many years ago, Yehoshua raised his arms and made the sun stand still in the sky. He did not want the day to end until the Jews had won the war they were fighting with their enemies.

...שֶׁמֶשׁ יָדַע מְבוֹאוֹ.

... The sun knows its destination — exactly when and where it will set.

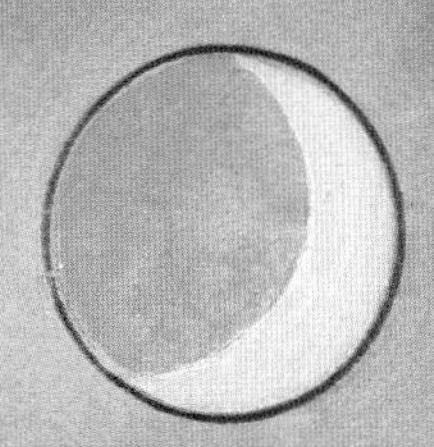

The sun is king of the day, but the moon rules the night. The sun is all fire and heat, but the moon is cold, hard rock. The moon has no light of its own; its light is reflected from the sun. So moonlight is really sunlight shining at night!

The moon is our heavenly calendar. It shows us the date of the Hebrew month and tells us when the festivals and holidays arrive. Each month, it travels around the earth. At first, it looks like a thin slice of light in the sky. Then it becomes a full, round circle. Then it grows small again. When the moon has almost disappeared, you know that *Rosh Chodesh*, the beginning of a new Hebrew month, is on its way.

עָשָׂה יָרֵחַ לְמוֹעֲדִים . . .

He made the moon to fix the times of the Festivals . . .

Look up at the sky again. Do you see the clouds? Clouds are like great, airy, floating baskets of water. When water evaporates from the earth and the sea, it rises in the air and forms clouds. Some clouds are white and puffy; some are flat and gray. Some are even almost black. But all clouds are blown around the earth by the wind, and all of them carry water. Clouds make the sky look pretty. And when the sun is hot and bright, clouds give us shade. What interesting shapes can you find in clouds?

During the forty years the Jews traveled in the desert, the *Ananey Hakavod* — G-d's Clouds of Glory — traveled with them and protected them from the heat of the sun and the cold of the night.

What a stormy day! The wind is busy pushing and shoving the clouds as giant sparks of lightning zigzag across the sky. They tear through the clouds, and with roars of thunder, rip them open and release the rain.

Big wet drops fall from the sky, drenching the thirsty forests and fields and splashing onto city sidewalks and streets. After a while, the clouds are empty and the storm ends. Sometimes it rains without storming. Then all you can hear is the soft pitter-patter of gently falling rain.

In the time of Noach, it rained for forty days and forty nights. The entire earth was covered with water. Only the people and animals in the ark were saved. They landed on a mountain, left the ark, and began to rebuild the world.

. . . הַשָּׂם עָבִים רְכוּבוֹ, הַמְהַלֵּךְ עַל כַּנְפֵי רוּחַ . . . מְשָׁרְתָיו אֵשׁ לֹהֵט.

. . . He makes the clouds His chariot. He walks on the wings of the wind . . . The flaming fire is His servant.

The other day, I saw a mountain for the first time. It was high and green and pointy at the top. Some mountains are round; some are covered with snow; others have forests on them. And some have holes at the top! These mountains are called volcanoes, and they shoot out streams of smoke and fiery lava. But all the mountains are like great bumps rising up from the ground and trying to reach the sky.

Hashem gave the Torah on a mountain — on Har Sinai — and the *Beis Hamikdash*, our Holy Temple in Jerusalem, was built on a mountain too. It's called Har Hamoriyah. It's the same mountain where Avraham Avinu brought his son Yitzchak for the *Akeidah*.

Lots of important things have happened to us on mountains. Maybe that's because people feel closer to Hashem when they climb up high. Then they can look out far and wide and see all the amazing things G-d made in the world!

יַעֲלוּ הָרִים . . .

They shall go up to the mountains . . .

But there are things to see in low places as well as on mountain tops. This is a valley. Valleys curve around and between the bottoms of mountains. They can be wide or narrow, big or small. They are good places to grow things because the rains bring rich, fertile soil down the mountain-sides, straight into the farms in the valley.

Emek Yizre'el — the Valley of Yizre'el — is the largest valley in the Land of Israel. It is filled with green orchards and thriving farms. *Emek* means "valley," and *Yizre'el* means "G-d will plant."

. . . יֵרְדוּ בְקָעוֹת . . .

. . . they shall go down to the valleys . . .

A river is a long stream of water flowing towards a lake or the sea. One river will rush madly on its way; another drifts lazily along, as if it had all the time in the world. Lazy rivers are good for going fishing or swimming. But every river brings the gift of water to the people who live along its shores.

The longest river in *Eretz Yisrael* is the *Yarden* — the Jordan River. It comes out of the ground in the north of the country and winds its way down south where it finally spills into the Dead Sea. When *Bnei Yisrael* were ready to enter the Land of Israel, Hashem stopped the flow of the Jordan River, so that the people could walk across on dry land.

הַמְשַׁלֵּחַ מַעְיָנִים בַּנְּחָלִים . . . יַשְׁקוּ כָּל חַיְתוֹ שָׂדָי . . .

He sends streams into the rivers . . . They bring water to all the animals in the fields.

Did you know that most of the earth is covered with water? Great oceans and seas divide the land. These oceans and seas are never empty. Rain from the clouds and water from the rivers keep them full.

The sea can be clear bright blue, or deep dark green, or dingy gray. It can be smooth and silky and still, or look like a giant roller coaster, with waves rising up and crashing down. But no matter what it looks like, sea water is always salty, and you cannot drink it.

Seas and oceans are full of marvelous living things — fish and plants that live inside the water; birds and animals that live above or around it. People can't live in the sea, but we can move across it on ships. It is our watery highway to faraway places all around the world.

When Yonah the Prophet tried to run away from G-d, he boarded a ship to the city of Nineveh. But Hashem sent a terrible storm to the ocean and a great fish to swallow Yonah, and Yonah realized there was no place he could hide from G-d, not even in the deep, dark sea!

זֶה הַיָּם גָּדוֹל וּרְחַב יָדָיִם . . . שָׁם אֳנִיּוֹת יְהַלֵּכוּן . . .

This is the sea; it is large and very wide . . . Ships will travel there . . .

A desert is dry, hot and dusty, the color of camels and sand. It is very hard for things to live in the desert, because there is very little water — no rivers or lakes, and hardly any rain at all.

Sometimes there are places in the desert with water and trees. These are called oases. An oasis is a green island in an ocean of sand.

The desert is a lonesome place to be. But Hashem is in the desert, just as He is everywhere else in the world. Avraham Avinu lived in the desert for many years. He pitched his tent near a desert road, and when travelers passed by, he invited them in and performed the *mitzvah* of *Hachnasas Orchim*. And of course the Jews lived in the desert for forty years when they came out of Egypt. They were able to live there because Hashem took special care of them. He gave them *mahn* to eat.

לְמוֹלִיךְ עַמּוֹ בַּמִּדְבָּר . . . (קלו:טז)

To Him Who leads His people through the wilderness . . .

The jungle is just the opposite of a desert. Although it too is hot, it is full of water, rivers and rain. It is shady and green and very wet. Because it has so much water, thousands upon thousands of creatures live in the jungle — from sleek tigers and huge elephants to glistening snakes, rainbow-colored birds, and flimsy, paper-thin butterflies. And no one has ever managed to count all the plants, trees, flowers and vines! The jungle is bursting with life.

The forest is home to many of the living things in the world. People build houses made of wood from the forest, but animals live inside the forest itself. Large animals, tiny ones, crawling insects, birds — all make their homes in, under and around the trees in the forest. And the forest feeds and protects them all.

It takes many years for a forest to grow, and it grows without any help from man. Each tree produces seeds that fall to the ground, take root and grow. Even

though we didn't plant the forests, we enjoy them. But if we are not careful, we can spoil or ruin them — by damaging the trees, or carelessly starting fires.

Shlomo Hamelech's palace was made out of cedar trees from Lebanon. It had so many beams of wood that it was called *Beis Ya'ar HaLevanon* — the House of the Forest of Lebanon.

יִשְׂבְּעוּ עֲצֵי ה׳, אַרְזֵי לְבָנוֹן אֲשֶׁר נָטָע.

G-d's trees are content and well cared for,
the Cedars of Lebanon which He has planted.

Waving yellow wheat or corn, green vines with tiny red tomatoes, round cotton plants with puffy white flowers . . . a field full of growing things is always a lovely sight to see.

A field means there is a farmer who worked hard plowing, planting, fertilizing, weeding, picking, and watering. Then, if all goes well, the long straight lines, or curvy circles, or nice neat squares he planted turn green and gold with growing things for us to eat. Isn't it an amazing thing that tiny seeds thrown into the soil can turn into food to keep us alive and healthy and well?

If the Jewish people keep the Torah and follow its laws, Hashem promised that the Land of Israel will give forth wondrous crops and provide us with everything we need.

מַצְמִיחַ חָצִיר לַבְּהֵמָה,
וְעֵשֶׂב לַעֲבֹדַת הָאָדָם, לְהוֹצִיא לֶחֶם מִן הָאָרֶץ.

He makes plants grow to feed the cattle. He makes crops grow so man can work and bring forth bread from the soil.

You can choose between hundreds of thousands of creatures that Hashem has created. Each one is absolutely amazing! And each one obeys Hashem and does just what it is supposed to do.

Do you remember the story of Bilaam and his donkey? The wicked Bilaam didn't listen to G-d, but the donkey did!

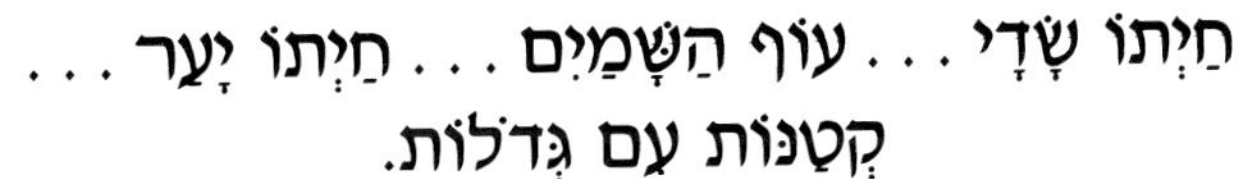

חַיְתוֹ שָׂדָי . . . עוֹף הַשָּׁמַיִם . . . חַיְתוֹ יָעַר . . .

קְטַנּוֹת עִם גְּדֹלוֹת.

Beasts of the field . . . birds of the heavens . . .
beasts of the forest . . . small creatures and large ones.

תְּשַׁלַּח רוּחֲךָ יִבָּרֵאוּן, וּתְחַדֵּשׁ פְּנֵי אֲדָמָה.

You shall send Your spirit and they shall be created again; You shall renew the face of the earth.

Summertime is growing time. In the summer everything is warm and green. Trees are heavy with ripe fruit; grasses and bushes and vines are flowering. The world is full of food for all the newborn.

... תִּפְתַּח יָדֶךָ יִשְׂבְּעוּן טוֹב.

... You open Your hand and all creatures are satisfied with Your goodness.

Autumn is harvest time, time to gather in the crops and to prepare for the coming winter. The newborn animals are old enough to care for themselves. The leaves on the trees turn orange and gold and begin to fall to the ground. The earth is slowing down for its annual rest. Autumn is a time to thank Hashem for a good year past. We celebrate the holiday of *Succos* in the autumn.

תִּתֵּן לָהֶם יִלְקֹטוּן . . .

You will give them food and they will gather it in.

Wintertime is cold. It is a time of crunchy snow to stomp on and make snowballs with. A time of boots and leggings and mittens. G-d's world is covered in white in the winter, frosted with chilly crystal made of ice. Isn't it amazing that the icy snow covers the roots of plants and trees and keeps them warm throughout the winter so the world can rest and sleep and wake up ready to grow again in the spring?

כֻּלָּם אֵלֶיךָ יְשַׂבֵּרוּן לָתֵת אָכְלָם בְּעִתּוֹ.

All the world waits for You to give them their food in due time.

Don't you agree that our world is a wonderful place to live in? That's why David Hamelech said . . .

מָה רַבּוּ מַעֲשֶׂיךָ, ה', כֻּלָּם בְּחָכְמָה עָשִׂיתָ,
מָלְאָה הָאָרֶץ קִנְיָנֶךָ.

How many great and wonderful things You have created, Hashem
You made them all with wisdom. The earth is full of Your work!